Elizabeth Vinson

MW01697788

Jude

THE PRACTICAL WAY TO LIVE IN THE MINGLING OF GOD WITH MAN

WITNESS LEE

Living Stream Ministry
Anaheim, CA • www.lsm.org

First Edition, September 2003.

ISBN 0-7363-2415-1

Published by

Living Stream Ministry
2431 W. La Palma Ave., Anaheim, CA 92801 U.S.A.
P. O. Box 2121, Anaheim, CA 92814 U.S.A.

Printed in the United States of America

03 04 05 06 07 08 09 / 9 8 7 6 5 4 3 2 1

CONTENTS

PREFACE

This book is composed of messages given by Brother Witness Lee at a conference in Reseda and Los Angeles, California, February 12-17, 1963. The conference consisted of six meetings; however, no record exists for Message Three. Consequently, this book contains only five chapters. These messages have not been reviewed by the speaker.

Chapter One

THE EIGHT STAGES OF THE CHRISTIAN LIFE IN ROMANS

Scripture Reading: Rom. 3:9, 20, 24; 5:11-12, 19; 6:3-6; 7:18; 8:2, 4-6, 28-29; 12:2-5

In this chapter I am burdened to speak concerning Paul's Epistle to the Romans. Readers of the book of Romans know quite well that this book reveals the stages of the Christian life. Among the sixty-six books of the Bible, it is this book that gives us a clear picture of the Christian life from its beginning to its maturity. If we are going to be normal and sound Christians, we have to know clearly the eight stages of the Christian life that are revealed to us in this book.

THE FIRST STAGE— SINFUL AND UNDER GOD'S CONDEMNATION

The first stage of the Christian life in the book of Romans is that of a man who is sinful and is condemned to death under the righteous judgment of God (1:1—3:20). This is the stage into which we were all born. Before we became Christians, we were sinful persons. As such, we were condemned to death by the righteous God. It was while we were in this stage that we became Christians.

THE SECOND STAGE— BEING JUSTIFIED AND REGENERATED

In the second stage, we see a man who has been justified through the redemption of Christ, has been accepted by God, and is now boasting because of the hope of the glory of God (3:21—5:11). Originally, this man was under the condemnation of God. Now, however, there is no more condemnation because he has been justified through Christ's redemption (3:24; cf. 5:16). As a result, this man has become a person who is full of joy and boasts because of the hope of the glory of God (v. 2). In this stage, we who were once under God's condemnation are saved, justified, and regenerated.

THE THIRD STAGE—REALIZING THAT IN ADAM WE HAVE SIN AND DEATH

In the third stage of the Christian life as seen in Romans, we see a saved and regenerated person who realizes that he was originally born in Adam and has thus inherited sin and death (5:12-21). After we have been born again, we may, perhaps very quickly, come to the point where we realize that because we were born in Adam, we are sinners and are destined to die. Coming to this realization is the third stage of the Christian life.

THE FOURTH STAGE—REALIZING THAT WE HAVE BEEN BAPTIZED INTO CHRIST

The sixth chapter of Romans presents to us the fourth stage of the Christian life. When we realize that we are in Adam and therefore have sin and death, we also realize that we have been baptized into Christ. Originally we were in Adam; now we are in Christ. We were born in Adam (cf. 5:17; 1 Cor. 15:22), but we have been baptized into Christ (Rom. 6:3; Gal. 3:27). On the day that we received the Lord Jesus as our personal Savior and were baptized, we were put into Christ. Whereas in Adam we received sin and death, in Christ we have righteousness and life (Rom. 5:17-18). Righteousness is versus sin, and life is versus death.

We as Christians have been not only regenerated but also transferred out of Adam into Christ. This transfer is similar to a transfer out of one house or building into another. We have "moved" out of Adam into Christ. We are no longer persons who are in Adam but persons who are in Christ. The old man, the old nature, and the old life have been crucified on the cross (Rom. 6:6; Gal. 2:20). They have been put to an end.

As long as you are a Christian, sooner or later there will

come a day when the Holy Spirit will make you realize the glorious fact that you, on the day of your baptism, were transferred out of Adam into Christ. I believe that when you see this glorious fact, you will say, "Hallelujah! Praise the Lord! I am now in Christ!" Our being in Christ is a glorious fact. Apparently, we are in Los Angeles or some other location, but actually we are in Christ. Christ is not only our life; He is our realm and our sphere (Rom. 8:1; Eph. 1:3). Sin and death were once our inheritance, but now we are in Christ, who is our sphere and our everything.

When the Lord revealed this glorious and precious fact to me in 1932, I was beside myself before God. I do not encourage you to try to repeat my experience. However, when you see the glorious fact that you are now in Christ, you will not be able to keep yourself silent. You will be beside yourself. You will say, "Hallelujah! Praise the Lord that I am now in Christ!" Although the phrase *in Christ* is composed of just two little words, the fact of being in Christ is not small. It would be good if you would frame those two words and hang them on your wall. Hallelujah! We are in Christ! What a glory!

THE FIFTH STAGE— TRYING TO DO GOOD IN THE FLESH

Although the fourth stage of the Christian life, seen in Romans 6, is a glorious one, the fifth stage, seen in chapter seven, is sorrowful. In chapter six, we declare, "Hallelujah!" but in chapter seven, we must cry out, "Wretched man that I am!" (v. 24). In this fifth stage, we see a man who strives and struggles to do good, to keep the law of God, and to please God by himself (vv. 18-19, 21-22). He does this because he now knows that he is in Christ. In a sense, he says to himself, "I am in Christ; therefore, I have to do good. Since I am now in Christ, I must keep the law. Because I am in Christ, I have to please God." Although it is true that he is in Christ, his thought that he must now do good is false. It is absolutely right to be in Christ, but to do good by oneself is one hundred percent wrong.

If you realize the fact that you are in Christ, you will

rejoice unceasingly. If, however, you make the decision to do good by yourself, you will be sorrowful. The reason for your sorrow will be that when you are trying to do good, you will in effect be "running away" from Christ. Of course, it is impossible to actually run away from Christ. But in experience, if you try to do good by yourself, you "run away" from Christ. If you try to do good by yourself, you will find that there is nothing good within you (v. 18). You must realize that you are nothing but flesh (v. 18), which can never do anything to please God (cf. 8:8). If therefore you try to do good by yourself, you will actually be living and walking in yourself, which means that you will be living and walking in the flesh and apart from Christ. It is for this reason that I ask you to give up any thought of doing good.

Yet herein lies a great temptation. When we rejoice that we are in Christ, the enemy often comes and subtly asks us whether or not we are in Christ. When we answer that we are indeed in Christ, he often challenges us, asking, "But do you do good? If you are in Christ, you must do your best to please God. You must make up your mind and make a decision to please God and keep His law." Although we may often think that such a thought is from the Holy Spirit, we must realize that it is nothing less than a temptation and a challenge from Satan himself. This temptation comes especially when we are in the midst of praising and thanking Christ that we are in Him. If we have learned this lesson well, we will tell Satan, "Get away from me, Satan. I will not go along with you. It is impossible for me to do good. I am flesh, and in my flesh nothing good dwells. Because there is nothing good in me, I cannot do any good thing. Satan, I have been fooled by you long enough; do not try to tempt me anymore. Get away from me!"

THE SIXTH STAGE—
WALKING ACCORDING TO THE SPIRIT

If we address the enemy in this way and reject trying to do good in the flesh, we will be persons who live and walk according to the Holy Spirit in our spirit. This is the stage that we see in Romans 8:1-17. Here we see a person who does not know good or evil and who has been released from doing good and evil; he simply knows to follow the Holy Spirit, who indwells his human spirit (v. 4; 1 Cor. 6:17).

In the garden of Eden, there were two trees—the tree of life and the tree of the knowledge of good and evil (Gen. 2:9). The second tree is not only a tree of the knowledge of evil; it is also the tree of the knowledge of good. Whenever you are trying to do good, you have to realize you are contacting the tree of the knowledge of good and evil. We are clear that evil opposes life, but we must be equally clear that good also opposes life. The tree of life is opposed by the tree of the knowledge of good and evil. Perhaps this thought has never occurred to you. Both good and evil are the enemies of Christ. Evil is against Christ. The same is true for good. Good is not Christ; good is against Christ. The Lord has no intention that we do good by ourselves. What the Lord asks us to do is not to do good but to follow Him, that is, to walk according to the Spirit who is in our spirit.

In Romans 7 we see a picture of a man trying to do good in his flesh, whereas in Romans 8 we see one who walks according to the Spirit in his human spirit. However, many Christians do not know the difference between doing good and walking according to the Spirit. Doing good is one thing; walking in the Spirit is entirely another. Yet many Christians think that doing good is synonymous with following the Holy Spirit and walking according to the Spirit. We must be delivered from doing good to walking according to the Spirit. For a number of years after I was saved, I prayed to the Lord every morning and made the decision to please Him by doing good. Yet despite my prayer and decisions, I simply could not make it. By the time evening came, I would have to go to the Lord to confess my failure and ask Him to cleanse me with His precious blood. When I experienced forgiveness and the cleansing of the precious blood, I would have peace in my conscience. The next morning, I would go to the Lord again and pray, "Lord, I praise You for this new day. I wish to have a new start. Lord, help me to do good." In other words, every day I made up my mind to do good, yet every day I would fail. Year after year I was in such a state—the state described in

Romans 7. Then one day the Lord opened my eyes to show me that there was no need for me to try to do good. He caused me to realize that I was in Christ, that the Holy Spirit was within me, and that consequently all I had to do was simply follow the Spirit. I realized that I did not have to make any more decisions to be good; I only had to go along with the Spirit. After I saw this, my morning prayer changed. I began to pray, "Praise You, Lord! Not only am I in You; Your Spirit is within me. There is nothing for me to do or to try to do. All I must do is simply enjoy and experience You. Hallelujah!"

We need to praise the Lord by saying "Hallelujah!" Sometimes the young people ask me what I do after I say "Hallelujah!" When Satan comes to tempt me, there is nothing for me to do but praise. I do not know anything except to say "Hallelujah!" We were not saved to do good; we were saved to praise, glorify, and thank the Lord (1 Thes. 5:16-18). We must remember that we are in Christ and that the Spirit of Christ is within us (Rom. 8:2, 9). Once we have such a realization, we must simply praise the Lord and say "Hallelujah!" all day long. There is nothing left for us to do except praise Him. One day when I spoke concerning this matter in a meeting, a sister came to me afterwards and said, "Brother Lee, I am very glad to have heard the message tonight. I realize what you mean when you tell us that we should say "Hallelujah!" But when I go back to my home, I will be met by my husband, who is a very hard man. What you say is very good, but what shall I do in my difficult situation?" I responded to her, "Sister, the harder your husband is, the more you have to say, 'Hallelujah!' Do not make up your mind to be patient. Do not try to do anything. The more you try to be patient, the more impatient you will be. Simply remember that whenever your husband is hard toward you, you must just say, 'Praise the Lord! Hallelujah!'" This is all we must do. For eternity we will say "Hallelujah!" A Christian is not someone who tries to do something; a Christian is a person who always enjoys and experiences Christ. We are not called by the Lord to do things to please Him. We are called to enjoy, experience, and participate in Christ. Never try to do good by yourself. Just remember that you are in Christ and that the Spirit of Christ is in you. If you need electricity, there is no need for you to do anything but turn on the switch. Saying "Hallelujah!" is the way to switch on to enjoy and experience Christ. If you try to be good by yourself, the switch will be turned off. Always remember to praise the Lord, for this is the way to switch on. This is the way to be a victorious person who is in Christ and walks according to the Spirit. We are set free from sin, death, and bondage simply by saying "Hallelujah!" and walking according to the Spirit.

THE SEVENTH STAGE— ALL THINGS WORKING TOGETHER FOR OUR CONFORMATION

The seventh stage of the Christian life as shown to us in Romans is the Lord arranging all things to work together for our good. This good can be considered as our profit, which is our conformation to the image of the firstborn Son of God. Romans 8:28-29 says, "And we know that all things work together for good to those who love God, to those who are called according to His purpose. Because those whom He foreknew, He also predestinated to be conformed to the image of His Son, that He might be the Firstborn among many brothers." By using all things—which include all environments, circumstances, and persons—as instruments, the Lord brings us into a situation of suffering, in which we can be conformed to His image.

In Romans 8:9 we are told that we have the Spirit of Christ within us. The "all things," however, are mainly outside of us. We can use the example of cooking to illustrate this. When we cook, we often use a pot. Within the pot, we put water; outside of the pot, there is fire. When we have the water within the pot and the fire outside of the pot, the food can be cooked. Many times we sense the Lord's presence within us as the Spirit and feel sweet. In addition, we frequently find ourselves in environments and circumstances that are akin to a burning fire. These environments are arranged by God in His sovereignty to work together for our good. The good spoken of here is our being conformed to the image of Christ. When the Lord arranges a wife for a husband or children for parents, the wife and the children work together for the husband's and parents' conformation. Throughout my forty years of Christian life, I have noticed that many times a brother whom it seems no one can help marries a precious wife who seems tailor-made to deal with him. According to the Lord's sovereign arrangement, a peculiar wife always will be able to deal with a peculiar husband and to work together for good for him. Everything is sovereign and everything is in the Lord's hand. He makes all things work together for our profit so that we will be conformed to the image of Christ. Hence, in the seventh stage, we see a person who is not only spiritual but who also bears the image of Christ. In those who are in this stage, we will be able to recognize the image, glory, expression, and manifestation of Christ.

THE EIGHTH STAGE— LIVING IN THE BODY OF CHRIST

The last picture of the Christian life in the book of Romans is contained in chapter twelve. This picture shows us one who is saved, walks according to the Spirit, is being conformed to the image of Christ, and is a member of the Body of Christ living in the Body of Christ and practicing the Body life. Such a one realizes that he is not an individual person but a member of the Body.

In this stage, we can see the daily Christian living, which is a living that is in the Body of Christ. Whatever we as Christians do, we must do as members of the Body of Christ. In this stage, we realize that we are no more independent and individual persons; we are but members of the Body of Christ. From the time we have this realization onward, we can never be independent or individualistic, because we are members of the Body. It is impossible for a member of my physical body to be independent. If a member of my physical body is independent, it is separate from the body and dies. Not only so, it becomes something that is dreadful and awful. The human hand is wonderful. Suppose, however, that my hand was separated from my body and put on a table. Surely this would be an awful situation. Today many believers are like separated members of a human body—they are not only dead; they are dreadful. This is because they are separated from the Body of Christ. The more we live as members in the Body of Christ, the more dear and beloved we are to the other members. Hence, in the last stage of the Christian life as seen in the book of Romans, we see the Body of Christ composed of all the saved ones who live in the Body mutually as members. This is the maturity of the Christian life.

In this message, we have covered the eight stages of the Christian life as seen in the Epistle to the Romans. In the first stage, we see a sinful person who is under the condemnation of God. The second stage presents to us a saved person—one who has been justified through the redemption of Christ. In the third stage, we see a person who, as a saved one, realizes that originally he was born in Adam. According to the fourth stage, we see how such a person realizes the fact that he is in Christ. The fifth stage presents to us a person who is fooled and tempted to try to do good by himself. In the sixth stage this person comes to know and realize that there is nothing left for him to do but to walk according to the Spirit. According to the seventh stage, this person accepts all the environments and circumstances from the sovereign hand of God for him to be conformed to the image of Christ. In the eighth and final stage, he realizes that he is a member of the Body of Christ and as such will never be independent or individualistic but will rather live, walk, act, and work as a member in the Body of Christ. We are no longer sinners in the world; we are members in the Body of Christ. As such, we must enjoy and experience Christ and walk, live, act, and work in the Body of Christ as His many members.

Chapter Two

HOW TO EXPERIENCE CHRIST IN A PRACTICAL WAY— FEEDING ON CHRIST AND DRINKING OF CHRIST

Scripture Reading: 1 Cor. 1:22-24; Col. 1:18-19; 2:2-3, 9; Eph. 3:8; Gal. 1:16; 2:20; 4:29; Eph. 3:17; Phil. 1:20-21; 1 Cor. 2:16; Matt. 16:24-25; Rom. 12:2; John 6:57

In the previous chapter, we fellowshipped concerning Christ being everything to us. We furthermore learned that when we realize the glorious fact that we are in Christ and Christ is in us, automatically we will be normal Christians. In this chapter, I feel burdened to fellowship more concerning this Christ who is in us and in whom we are. Although we know that Christ is life and everything to us, we have to know more particularly who Christ is and how we can experience Him practically.

THE FULLNESS OF THE GODHEAD AND THE UNSEARCHABLE RICHES OF CHRIST

Christ is the embodiment of God. Colossians 2:9 says, "For in Him dwells all the fullness of the Godhead bodily." We can explain what the fullness of the Godhead is in a very simple way. God is love, so love is an item of the fullness of the Godhead. God is also light, so light is an item of the fullness of the Godhead. Moreover, God is power and life, so power and life are items of the fullness of the Godhead. Furthermore, because God is holiness and righteousness, these are also items of the fullness of the Godhead. This fullness—the fullness of the Godhead—dwells in Christ bodily. Hence, because everything of God is in Christ, Christ is the embodiment of God. It is impossible to experience God without Christ;

outside of Christ, we can never contact God in a practical way. Everything that God has and is dwells in Christ.

Not only so, from Colossians 1:18-19 we also know that God's desire, intention, and eternal plan is to give the first place to Christ in everything because God's pleasure is to have all His fullness dwell in Christ. Christ must have the first place, that is, the preeminence, in everything. In God's heart, mind, desire, intention, and eternal plan, there is nothing but Christ Himself. God put everything of Himself into Christ, made Christ to be everything in His purpose, and gave Him the first place. Such a Christ is surely beyond our imagination. Hence, the apostle Paul told us that what he preached was the "unsearchable riches of Christ" (Eph. 3:8). The riches of Christ are unsearchable; that is, they are endless. This is the Christ in whom we are and who is in us.

KNOWING AND EXPERIENCING CHRIST AS FOOD AND DRINK

Although it may be easy to understand such a Christ and to speak of the unsearchable riches of Christ doctrinally, it is difficult to experience Him in a practical way. Practically speaking, what aspects of Christ have we experienced? It is one thing to say that Christ is unsearchably rich; it is quite another to actually experience this Christ. I once counted 277 aspects of Christ in the Bible. We need to experience Christ in each of these aspects. But in particular, we need to practically experience Christ as two things—food and drink.

Christ is the bread of life and the living water (John 6:35; 7:38). In John 6:57 the Lord said to His disciples, "As the living Father has sent Me and I live because of the Father, so he who eats Me, he also shall live because of Me." It is not enough for us to simply realize that Christ is food to us; we have to eat Him. We must not only realize that He is the living water to us; we must drink Him. The Lord emphasizes in this verse that we must actually eat Him. Frequently I want to ask the young people, "How much have you enjoyed Christ today? Did you feed on Him? Did you drink of Him?" We should not say that Christ is food and drink to us yet not practically enjoy Him daily as such. I have found that many people do not know how to feed on Christ and drink of Him. They know that Christ is food and drink to them, and they know that they are in Christ and that Christ is in them. Nevertheless, they neither know how to feed on Christ nor how to drink of Him. They know so much, but they cannot bring their knowledge into practice. We need to know how to enjoy and experience Christ in our daily life. Christ is food and drink to us, and we must know how to eat and drink Him.

God's eternal desire is that He would mingle Himself with us to make each of us a God-man. God's intention is to make each of us not merely a man of God but a God-man—a man who is mingled with God. We can illustrate very simply how God can be mingled with us. In order for anything to be mingled with us, it has to be eaten by us. When we eat something, that thing mingles with us and becomes our element and a part of us. When a typical American man is fully grown, he may weigh two hundred pounds and stand over six feet tall. The way that this man became so big was by eating the produce of America over the course of many years. After eating the meats, fruits, and vegetables of America, he is, in a strict sense, a constitution of American food. Because this man has eaten and digested this food, it is mingled with him and has become his element.

We have an imbalanced idea of what God is to us. We frequently think that God is high, great, and far-off from us. Our idea is that we must bow down and prostrate ourselves before Him. This is a mistaken concept. The Scriptures tell us clearly that immediately after God created man, He presented Himself to man in the form of the tree of life (Gen. 2:9). God came to man as the tree of life not to be outwardly worshipped by man but to be eaten by man. One day God came to this world in the form of a man (John 1:1, 14). When He was on the earth, a woman addressed Him as "Lord, Son of David" (Matt. 15:22). The Lord responded by telling her that He was "the children's bread" (v. 26). While the woman called Him "Lord, Son of David," He identified Himself as bread. In the Gospel of John, Christ is God incarnated. Yet He told us that He is the bread of life for us to eat and the living water for us to drink. According to our concept, God is mighty, glorious, great, and very far from us. However, God's intention and desire is that He would be food that we would take and eat. The more we eat Him, the more pleased He will be. The best worship, the real worship, and the worship that the Father seeks is enjoying God (cf. 4:14, 23-24). God's eternal intention is to make Himself food to us so that He can be eaten and digested by us and thereby be mingled with us. God is in Christ (Col. 2:9), who is our true food and drink. Everything of God is in Christ, Christ is the Spirit (2 Cor. 3:17), and now the Spirit is in us.

THE RESULT OF EATING CHRIST

When we eat Christ, He as the Spirit comes into us and operates in a number of ways.

Christ Revealed in Us

First, the Spirit reveals Christ in us. Galatians 1:16 includes the phrase *to reveal His Son in me.* The more we are filled with the Holy Spirit, the more we will sense the presence of Christ. Christ dwells within us, but it is because the Holy Spirit is within us that we know this. Radio waves bring messages to us which we receive and play on the radio. As long as we have the radio waves, we have the message, because the radio waves contain the message and bring it to us. The radio waves in this example signify the Holy Spirit. With the Holy Spirit there is the presence of Christ. As long as we have the Holy Spirit indwelling us, we have the presence of Christ within us. Hence, the Holy Spirit reveals Christ to us. Our experience confirms that whenever we are filled with the Holy Spirit, we feel Christ's presence. Not only so, but the more we are filled with the Holy Spirit, the more we sense the glorious presence of Christ. This is because the Holy Spirit reveals Christ in our spirit.

Christ Living in Us

Second, Christ lives in us as the Spirit. When the Spirit indwells us, Christ lives in us, for Christ is the Spirit (2 Cor. 3:17). Galatians 2:20 tells us that Christ lives in us. This Christ lives in us to be our life (Col. 3:4) that we may live by

Him. Because we are regenerated, we possess two different kinds of lives—the natural life and Christ Himself as life. Since Christ is life to us and since He lives within us, we must daily live by Christ and not by the natural life.

Christ Being Formed in Us

Third, the Spirit works within us so that Christ is formed in us. In Galatians 4:19 Paul writes, "My children, with whom I travail again in birth until Christ is formed in you." We can use the example of an egg to understand what is meant by the word *formed.* If we place a fertilized egg in an incubator and observe the egg day by day by holding it up to the light, over a period of time we will see a chick form within the egg. At our regeneration, Christ came into us as a seed (1 Pet. 1:23). Now He needs to be formed within us. It is not enough that Christ has been revealed in us and now lives within us—He must be formed in us. For Christ to be formed in us means that He becomes everything to our entire being. When Christ is formed within us, our whole soul—mind, emotion, and will—is full of Christ. This is why 1 Corinthians 2:16 says that we have the mind of Christ. This is a mind that Christ fills until it is full of Him, a mind in which Christ is formed. Many times we can tell just by the way a person thinks that his mind is full of Christ and that Christ occupies his mind. It is the same with the emotion. When Christ occupies the emotion of a person, whatever he loves is what Christ loves. Likewise with the will, whatever a man who has Christ formed within him chooses or decides, we sense that with him is the presence of Christ.

Christ Making Home in Our Hearts

Christ being formed in us is very much related to Christ making home in our hearts (cf. Eph. 3:17). Our heart is a composition of the three parts of our soul—the mind, emotion, and will—plus one part of our spirit, the conscience (Matt. 9:4; John 16:22; Acts 11:23; Heb. 10:22). For Christ to make home in our heart simply means that Christ occupies all the parts of our heart. It is not enough for us to declare how glorious it is that we are in Christ and how sweet it is that Christ is in us. We have to realize that Christ wants to make home in every part of our heart; this will give Him the ground to occupy our whole being.

The simple way to give the Lord the ground to make home in our hearts is to deny ourselves. In Matthew 16:24-25 the Lord Jesus says, "If anyone wants to come after Me, let him deny himself and take up his cross and follow Me. For whoever wants to save his soul-life shall lose it; but whoever loses his soul-life for My sake shall find it." To deny the self means to lose the soul-life, that is, the natural life. The terms *self, soul, natural man,* and *old man* are, for the most part, synonymous in that they all relate to one thing—the old life, the natural life. We have to deny our soul-life; that is, we have to deny our natural mind, natural emotion, and natural will. If we deny the self, that is, the soul-life, and put it to death, we will give Christ the ground to take over and possess our mind, emotion, and will and thereby make home in our heart. At that point, all the parts of our heart will be full of Christ, and we will have the mind, emotion, and will of Christ. To deny the natural life of the mind, emotion, and will and let Christ occupy all the parts of our being is to live by Christ, take Christ as our life, let Christ live in us, and take Christ as everything in a very practical way.

It is easy to say that we are in Christ, that Christ is in us, and that Christ is everything to us, but we need to experience these things in a practical way. When we are in the midst of thinking, we must reject our natural mind. When we love something or someone, we must give up the natural emotion and deny the self. When we make choices, we must deny the self and reject our natural will. In all the parts of our heart, we need to give Christ the first place. Unless we deny the self, bear the cross, and put our natural life to death, it will be impossible for us to live by Christ and take Him as our life. The way to take Christ as our life in a practical way is to reject the natural mind, emotion, and will.

I ask you to practice this matter day by day. When you think about a certain thing, remember that you are a Christian and have Christ living in you. As such, you must deny your self and reject your natural mind. By doing this, you yield your mind to Him. When you love something or someone, remember that you have Christ living in you, and deny your self, rejecting your natural emotion. To do this is to yield your emotion to Christ and let Him occupy it. We must do the same in regard to the natural will. We have to reject our self and let Christ occupy our entire being, thereby allowing Him to make home in our hearts completely.

Christ is real, living, and active. This active One is in you, waiting to occupy your whole being. But He can do this only if you give Him the opportunity. If you give Him the ground, He will take and occupy it. As a result, you will experience Him as life moment by moment, He will be gradually formed in you, and you will be conformed to the image of Christ.

Christ Being Manifested through Us, and Our Living Christ

When Christ is formed in us, whenever we think, love, or decide, we will have the image of Christ and bear the expression of Christ. This means that spontaneously Christ will be magnified through us and our life, being, and doing will be an expression, a manifestation, of Christ (Phil. 1:20-21). To have this kind of living is to live Christ. This is the Christian daily living.

THE PRACTICAL WAY TO EAT AND DRINK CHRIST—READING THE WORD AND PRAYING IN THE SPIRIT

The Christian daily living is a living of experiencing Christ in a practical way. As we have seen, enjoying Christ as food and drink is vital to the practical experience of Christ in a daily way. However, we may not know how to eat and drink Christ. We as Christians are familiar with many spiritual terms. Yet when we are pressed to give exact definitions of these terms and to testify concerning our experience of them, we frequently realize that we know very little. Hence, although we know that Christ is food and drink to us, very few of us know how to enjoy Him as such. We need to know practically how to enjoy Christ as food and drink.

We drink Christ by praying and we eat Him by contacting His word. The Lord is the Spirit (2 Cor. 3:17). The best way to contact the Spirit is by praying. When we pray, we are exercising our spirit, and when we exercise our spirit, our spirit contacts the Holy Spirit (John 4:24; Rom. 8:16; Eph. 6:18). The more we pray, the more we exercise our spirit and contact the Spirit with our spirit. Since the Spirit is the living water (John 7:38-39), at the very moment we are praying, we are drinking the living water. Although praying is the main way to drink Christ, we drink Him any time that we exercise our spirit to contact the Holy Spirit.

The Lord is not only the Spirit for us to drink by prayer; He is also the Word for us to eat (John 1:1; Rev. 19:13; John 5:39-40). Whenever we contact the Word with our spirit, we feed on the Lord. In John 6:57 the Lord says, "As the living Father has sent Me and I live because of the Father, so he who eats Me, he also shall live because of Me." When the disciples heard this, many of them reacted, saying, "This word is hard; who can hear it?" (v. 60). Surely they were trying to understand how the Lord could give them His flesh so that He could be eaten by them. Then in verse 63 the Lord said, "It is the Spirit who gives life; the flesh profits nothing; the words which I have spoken to you are spirit and are life." The Lord told His disciples to take Him as their food, but He was not referring to His physical flesh. Rather, it is the Spirit who gives life, and the words that He had spoken to them were spirit and life. According to these verses, taking Christ's words is the same as taking Him as our food. The Lord's words are to be taken not just in the mind but in the spirit. If we take the word of God only in the mind, it will be merely doctrine and teaching. However, if we take the word in our spirit, it will become food (Jer. 15:16).

If we are to enjoy Christ as food and drink, we have to take the word and pray in our spirit. When we pray to the Lord in our spirit, we are drinking the Lord as the living water. When we contact the word with our spirit, we are feeding on the Lord as our food. Day by day we have to learn how to experience and enjoy Christ by contacting the word and praying in our spirit. When we do, we will experience the Lord's energizing power by which we can live, think, love, choose, and act.

The breakfast that we eat every morning is the strengthening and energizing power within us by which we can live throughout the day. In the same way, we have to come to the Lord every morning and eat and drink of Him moment by moment. We also need to come to Him to contact His word and to pray to Him in our spirit. The more we contact His word and pray to Him in our spirit, the more we will feed on Him and drink of Him and thus experience Him as our life, energy, and strength by which we can live as a normal Christian. If we eat and drink Him by reading and praying, we will think by Christ, love by Christ, decide by Christ, and have a life that is fully in Christ. Such a life of eating and drinking Christ is a life of enjoying and experiencing Christ as everything to us in a practical way.

Chapter Three

THE MINGLING OF GOD WITH MAN

Scripture Reading: Lev. 2:4; 1 Cor. 6:17; Rom. 8:4-6, 16

There is a mystery revealed in the Scriptures that we can never comprehend fully. This mystery, which is revealed to us throughout the entire Bible, is the mingling of God with man. Among Christians today the term *mingling,* particularly as it relates to the mingling of God with man, is rarely used. This term was adopted by us from Leviticus 2:4, which says, "And when you present an offering of a meal offering baked in the oven, it shall be of fine flour, unleavened cakes mingled with oil or unleavened wafers anointed with oil." In the Scriptures oil signifies the Holy Spirit of God, and fine flour signifies the human nature—particularly that of Christ. Hence, in Leviticus 2:4 we see the mingling of the Holy Spirit with the human nature. This is the mingling of God with man.

The relationship between God and man in its highest aspect is one of mingling. Indeed, God's intention and desire is to mingle Himself with us. However, this thought may be rather difficult for us to realize. According to our natural thought, God is God and man is man—He is our Creator and we are His creatures. We have always believed that we as God's creatures could but worship, serve, and fear Him. Unless we have received revelation, we have perhaps never had the thought that God mingles Himself with man. While it is true that the Scriptures speak concerning the worship of God, many people are preoccupied with this matter according to their natural concept. If we read the Scriptures carefully without any human concepts or ideas about the nature of our fellowship with God, we will realize that God's intention has much more to do with our being mingled with Him than it does with our outwardly worshipping Him.

EATING AND MINGLING

In the previous chapter, we pointed out that after God created man, He came to man not as the high and glorious God to be worshipped but as the tree of life to be eaten. In the natural mind the thought that God's intention is to be partaken of by us as food does not exist. Before I saw this picture as a revelation, my thought had always been that God is so glorious, high, great, and holy, and we as men must worship, serve, and, at the very most, love Him. God's intention is not mainly that He would be worshipped by man; His intention is that man would take Him as food. The entire Bible speaks of this. In the Scriptures both the first and last pictures that reveal the relationship between God and man show us that God is to be partaken of by us. The first picture in the Scriptures that shows us the relationship between God and man is that of God making Himself available as the tree of life to be partaken of by man (Gen. 2:9). The last picture in the Scriptures is the same—the tree of life growing on both sides of the river of water of life, which flows from the throne (Rev. 22:1-2). These pictures show us that God's intention is that He would be mingled with us. Just as our food is mingled with us through our eating and digestion of it, in order for God to fulfill His intention of being mingled with us, He must be eaten by us.

This is not my word; it is the word of the Lord Jesus Himself. He tells us in John 6 that He is the bread of life which came down out of heaven (vv. 48, 51). In verse 57 the Lord tells us, "He who eats Me, he also shall live because of Me." In this verse, the Lord Jesus tells us emphatically that we can eat Him. While it is true that the Lord's word bears some symbolic meaning, the word *eat* is very strong and definite in its meaning. Because the Lord is bread, we have to eat Him and take Him as food. Not only so, in chapters four and seven, the Lord tells us that if we are thirsty, we can come to Him and drink Him as the living water (4:14; 7:37). According to John 1:12-13, to believe into the Lord simply means to receive

Him. Throughout the Gospel of John, the Lord constantly tells men to believe into, that is, to receive, Him (8:24; 9:35; cf. 10:25-26; 14:1; 17:20). The way we receive the Lord is the same way we receive food and water—eating and drinking. God is in the form of food so that He can be eaten and digested by man to become man's element.

I am burdened to share these things with you because the truth and mystery of the entire Word of God is centered on the mingling of God with man. If you do not see the mingling of God with man, it will be difficult for you to understand the mystery of the Scriptures. God is love (1 John 4:16), yet how do we enjoy God's love and express it to others? The only way is to be mingled with God. Without mingling with God, we can never enjoy God's love in a subjective way and we can never share God's love with others. God is also light (1:5). The way that we enjoy God and allow God's light to shine through us is by being mingled with God. The mingling is the key to unlocking the mystery of the relationship between God and us.

God is in Christ, Christ is the Spirit, and the Spirit is in us to do the work of mingling God with us (Col. 2:9; 2 Cor. 3:17; Rom. 8:11). The more the Holy Spirit works within us, the more we are mingled with God. First Corinthians 6:17 says, "But he who is joined to the Lord is one spirit." The expression "one spirit" indicates the mingling of the Lord as the Spirit with our spirit. Our spirit has been regenerated by the Spirit of God (John 3:6), who is now in us (1 Cor. 6:19) and is one with our spirit (Rom. 8:16). This is the realization of the Lord who became the life-giving Spirit through resurrection (1 Cor. 15:45; 2 Cor. 3:17) and who is now with our spirit (2 Tim. 4:22). This mingled spirit is often referred to in Paul's Epistles, as in Romans 8:4-6. This is the mingling of two persons—God and us—into one.

JESUS CHRIST—THE MINGLING OF GOD WITH MAN

Jesus Christ is the mingling of God with man. When He was on this earth, He was both man and God—He was the God-man. Even today, He is both a genuine man and the very God. God cannot be separated from Him. Once tea is mingled with water, wherever the water is, the tea is also. Just as tea is mingled with water, so also God is mingled with humanity in Christ. Wherever Christ is, God is as well. Stephen's word in Acts 7 proves that even after His ascension into heaven, the Lord Jesus is not only God but also a man: "Behold, I see the heavens opened up and the Son of Man standing at the right hand of God" (v. 56). There is a man in the heavens who is the embodiment of God. Before Christ was born in Bethlehem, God and man were separate. At the incarnation, however, God and man were joined as one in Christ. God is no longer merely God—He in Christ is mingled with man. It is here that the belief of Christians differs from the Jewish belief. According to the Jews, God is merely God (*Elohim*); Christians believe that this God is not only God but also God incarnated to be a man. Like the Jews, we believe that God is the Creator and the Lord. But unlike them, we believe that Jesus Christ is the Lord. The Lord God and the Lord Jesus are not two Lords but one. Christ Jesus the Lord is the Creator God incarnated to be mingled with man. The Lord Jesus Christ is a man who, on the day of His ascension, was exalted to heaven and established by God to be the Lord. Acts 2:36 says, "Therefore let all the house of Israel know assuredly that God has made Him both Lord and Christ, this Jesus whom you have crucified." If Christ were merely God, there would be no need in the Bible for such a verse. However, since Christ is a mingling of God and man, He in His humanity needed to be made the Lord and Christ.

In speaking of Christ being a mingling of God with man, we are not implying that a third nature was produced. Incarnation brought divinity into humanity and made them one entity, but neither divinity nor humanity was changed in nature. No; divinity remains divinity, and humanity remains humanity. This is illustrated by the mingling of oil with fine flour in the meal offering. The oil and the flour are mingled together to form one entity with two natures. However, each nature remains separate and complete. The oil does not lose its nature, and the flour does not change its nature. Nevertheless, the oil and the flour are mingled together to produce one entity. This entity is not a third nature, something that is neither oil nor flour. Rather, it is a complete entity with two natures, the nature of oil and the nature of flour. This is an illustration of incarnation bringing divinity into humanity, making them one, and causing them to live as one.

THE BELIEVERS—THE MINGLING OF GOD WITH MAN

The Lord Jesus Christ was the first mingling of God with man, and everyone who has been reborn and regenerated is a reproduction of Christ as a mingling of God with man. Christians are simply the mingling of God with man. A thorough realization of this vital point will solve all the problems in the Christian life, for every part of the Christian life is in reality a part of the mingling of God with man.

It is crucial to realize that Adam in his pre-fallen state was not a mingling of God with man. After Adam was formed of the dust of the earth, he was only a creature of God—he was not the mingling of God with man. However, if Adam and Eve had eaten of the tree of life, which was the manifestation of God, then they would have been mingled with God. After God created man, God presented Himself in the form of the tree of life to be partaken of by man. However, Satan came in, frustrated man from eating of the tree of life, and tempted him to take the tree of the knowledge of good and evil instead. As a result, the tree of life was closed to man by God with cherubim and a flaming sword (Gen. 3:24). This means that the God who is life to man was closed off from man by His glory, holiness, and righteousness. Unless the requirements of God's glory, holiness, and righteousness were met, the way for man to touch God as life would remain closed. This, in type, is the veil that separated us from God (Exo. 26:31; Rom. 3:23; cf. 1 Cor. 6:11; Rom. 3:10). Christ's death met all the requirements of God's glory, holiness, and righteousness, and as a result, the veil in the temple was rent, and the way to contact God as life was opened (Matt. 27:51; Heb. 10:19-20). Because He opened the living way, we can boldly come forward in the blood of Jesus to contact God as our life directly.

The God with whom we are mingled is the Triune God Himself—the Father, the Son, and the Spirit. The Father is the fountain, the Son is the spring, and the Holy Spirit is the stream (Psa. 36:9; John 4:14; 7:37; 2 Cor. 13:14; Rev. 22:1). Not only is God flowing out for us to drink of Him as the Spirit; He also created a spirit within us (Zech. 12:1). Consequently, when God as the Spirit flows into us, He flows into our spirit and mingles with our spirit as one spirit. First Corinthians 6:17 testifies of this mingling: "But he who is joined to the Lord is one spirit."

THE MINGLING OF GOD WITH MAN BEING THE KEY TO THE SCRIPTURES

After forty years of studying the Bible, I can say with assurance that if we do not realize the mingling of God with man, we can never understand the Scriptures thoroughly. The key to all the parables, types, prophecies, admonitions, teachings, doctrines, and truths in the Bible is the mingling of God with man. Without this key, even if we seemingly understand the Bible, our understanding is superficial. We cannot understand the Bible deeply until we touch the mingling of God with man. Because this is the key, it is possible to see this mingling in any part of the Scriptures. For example, 1 Corinthians 3:16 says, "Do you not know that you are the temple of God, and that the Spirit of God dwells in you?" The temple of God is the mingling of God with man. The temple itself, humanity, is the container, and the One who comes into the temple to dwell there, God Himself, is the content. Hence, the real meaning of the temple of God is the mingling of God with man. By this we can see that the key to unlocking the Bible is the mingling of God with man.

THE PRACTICAL WAY TO BE MINGLED WITH GOD

In order to participate practically in the mingling of God with man, we must know how to exercise our spirit and deny our soul-life. Genuine spirituality and the mingling of God with man can be realized by us only in the spirit; it cannot be realized in the soul. Nevertheless, most Christians are taught and trained to exercise their mind; rarely are they taught how to exercise their spirit. As a result, although people may understand doctrines, they may not know how to enter into the experience of these doctrines in their spirit. Take for example the matter of taking Christ as our food and drink.

Although some may understand this matter as a teaching or doctrine in the mind, very few know how to exercise their spirit to eat and drink Christ practically. Hence, we must learn how to exercise our spirit that God has formed within us. The exercise of the spirit is not mere doctrine; it is the practical way to eat and drink Christ and thus be mingled with God.

The way to exercise our spirit is to deny our self—the natural mind, emotion, and will. In our daily life we constantly encounter situations that expose our need to deny the self and exercise the spirit. If you are a man from China, you were raised in a certain way and have a particular way of doing things. Another brother, however, may be from the United States and consequently does things the American way. If you and the American brother are in the self and have to coordinate to do something, there will be friction. In your emotion, you will not be happy with the other brother, and in your mind, you will not agree with some of the things he does. If you are to take Christ as your life, you cannot go along with your emotion and mind. If you cling to your natural mind and emotion, that is an indication that you are still living by your natural life and are not taking Christ as your life. You must deny the self, including the mind, emotion, and will. It is good in such situations to declare to the self, "I am a reborn person. Christ dwells within my spirit and He is my life. Mind, I will not live by you. Emotions, I will not go along with you. Christ lives in my spirit, and I will go along with my spirit." This is to deny the self and reject the natural life. In so doing, you give the Holy Spirit within your spirit an opportunity to take over, saturate, and renew your mind, emotion, and will, transforming them from being natural to being Christ's. When we turn to our spirit, the Holy Spirit strengthens us into our inner man to reject the natural life.

My burden is not to give you more knowledge and doctrine; my burden is to help you know how to exercise your spirit, where God and man are mingled. There are two ways to live our lives. The first is to merely imitate what the Lord did. The second is to receive Him as our life and then let Him live in us. It is one thing to imitate Christ; it is another thing entirely for this very Jesus to come into us, mingle with us, and be our life. It is impossible for us to do what He did and be what He was by imitation. Even if such an imitation were somehow possible, it would be a false imitation. The outward imitation of Christ is not the genuine Christian life. The real Christian life is one of mingling with Christ by both exercising our spirit to eat and drink Him and denying the self. This is the practical way to live in the mingling of God with man.

Chapter Four

DENYING THE NATURAL MIND, EMOTION, AND WILL TO GO ALONG WITH THE INDWELLING CHRIST

Scripture Reading: Rom. 8:29; 1 Cor. 6:17; 2 Cor. 3:16-18; Rom. 12:2; Eph. 3:17a; 1 Cor. 2:16

Romans 8:29 tells us that God predestinated us to be conformed to the image of His Son. This is the desire of God's heart. The Scriptures tell us that originally God had the only begotten Son, the Lord Jesus Christ (John 1:18). The Bible also tells us that after the death and resurrection of Christ, God had many sons, with Christ as the Firstborn among them (cf. 20:17; Heb. 2:10; cf. Rom. 8:29). In other words, Christ was originally the only begotten Son of God, but after He died and rose from the dead, He became the Firstborn of many sons.

God's work according to His eternal purpose is to produce many sons with His Firstborn as the model. God's firstborn Son is the pattern, and according to this pattern, this model, He has produced many sons. God has accomplished this through our regeneration. When we received the Lord Jesus as our Savior, the Holy Spirit entered into our spirit. Because the Spirit is the reality of Christ, when the Spirit came into us, Christ Himself came into us. Now, by virtue of our having been regenerated, Christ is in us. Before Christ came into our spirit, our spirit was dead because of sin (Eph. 2:1, 5). However, Christ is life, and when He entered into us, He enlivened our deadened spirit. Because He as the Spirit has entered into our spirit, He is now our life (Col. 3:4). It is by the Spirit regenerating us with Christ as life that we have been made God's many sons. Not only so, God put His Son into us so that Christ would grow and be formed within us (Gal. 4:19). This fulfills God's eternal purpose and desire that we would be His sons in life, nature, and image.

I have been a believer for thirty-eight years. For the first years of my Christian life I was taught much and heard many messages. Within four and a half years I listened to more than one thousand messages. Not only was I taught much in the meetings, but I also read many Christian books. These messages, teachings, and books stressed mainly negative matters, such as how to overcome sin, pride, hatred, and falsehood. During those first years, I do not recall ever being taught that, on the positive side, God's eternal purpose is that we would be conformed to the image of His Son. The teaching on the negative side, however, never enabled me to overcome these matters. The more I tried, the more frustrated I became, that is, until after a period of time, when I gave up trying altogether. It was then that the Lord opened my eyes to realize that there is no need for me to try to do anything. I realized that since the Holy Spirit was within me, He would work out my conformation to His glorious image. When I realized this, I forgot about trying to be humble and trying not to be proud.

We should forget about these negative matters. The more we try to deal with them, the more we will be troubled by them. For example, the more we try to be humble, the prouder we will become. God did not ordain us to live in such a way. Rather, He foreordained us to be conformed to the image of Christ. We have to focus on Christ and forget about sin. However, it is very hard for us to do this. As Christians, we constantly remember that we should not sin, that we should be humble, and that we should not do anything wrong. Consequently, it is very hard for us to forget about these negative things. It is God's desire that we be conformed to the image of Christ. Let us therefore forget about doing good or evil. We should tell good and evil, "I have nothing to do with you anymore. I only care for Christ. Christ is my aim and my everything. I need to be conformed to the image of Christ. He is now in me as the Spirit. He is also my life. I no longer pay attention to good and evil. I only know to live by Christ who is my life."

APPLYING CHRIST

Our problem is that although Christ is in us, we do not apply Him. When I was a young man in China, I used oil lamps for light. Even after electricity was installed in my house, by force of habit I would often strike a match and light the oil lamp when I returned home at night. Even though I tried to remember that since I had electricity, I no longer needed to use the oil lamp, I would frequently forget. At the time of our regeneration, Christ came into us as an "electric lamp." Nevertheless, because we are so accustomed to our "oil lamp," that is, our old life, we forget to apply Christ in our daily living. In other words, although we have been regenerated in our spirit, we still remain in the old life and forget to live by Christ. This is an indication that after we have been regenerated, we still need to be transformed.

Transformation is very important. Yet among the children of God today, it is almost entirely neglected. Christians speak very much concerning sanctification and holy living. However, our being transformed is more vital than our being sanctified, for unless we are transformed, we cannot be sanctified. We must be transformed from the old life, form, and shape into another life, form, and shape. The old form is the form of Adam. The new form is the form of Christ. To be regenerated is one thing; to be transformed is another thing. Although we have been regenerated in our spirit, the remainder of our being—primarily our mind, emotion, and will—has yet to be transformed. Hence, we are still in the old man.

We are certain that our spirit is regenerated, but are we as confident that our mind, emotion, and will have been transformed? Are all these parts transformed, or do they remain in the old life? We all must admit that there is still a way for us to go before we are fully transformed in our soul. In Romans 12:2 Paul uses the phrase *be transformed by the renewing of the mind.* This verse implies that although we have been regenerated in our spirit, our mind remains old. Our mind is about six thousand years old—it is the mind of Adam. Hence, our mind, and with it our emotion and will, stands in need of being transformed.

How then can we be transformed? This matter has much to do with our heart. Ephesians 3:17 speaks of Christ making home in our hearts. Again, we have all been regenerated, but I doubt that Christ has made His home in many of our hearts. Is your heart Christ's home? Does Christ really make His home in your heart? Do you love the Lord so much that you offer your heart to Him to let Him occupy it fully? This is a vital matter. The Lord already dwells in our spirit. The problem is whether or not Christ is making home in our heart. The spirit and the heart are not the same. The Scriptures tell us that the heart includes all the parts of the soul—the mind, emotion, and the will (Matt. 9:4; John 16:22, 6; Heb. 4:12)—plus the conscience (10:22; 1 John 3:20). Although we have been regenerated in our spirit, we have to be transformed in our mind, emotion, and will. This transformation can take place only when Christ occupies our heart as a home. We have to love Christ with our whole heart, offer our heart to Him, and let Him take over our whole heart so that He may dwell in it. We should tell Him, "Lord, here is my heart. Come and occupy it fully. Come to make home in my heart."

First Corinthians 2:16 says, "For who has known the mind of the Lord and will instruct Him? But we have the mind of Christ." That we have the mind of Christ means that our mind has been transformed into the mind of Christ. We have Christ, but we have Him in our spirit only. Whether or not Christ occupies our mind, emotion, or will is the problem. If we are going to enjoy and experience Christ, we must learn this lesson absolutely. We have to love the Lord with our whole heart, offer our whole heart to Him, and give up our mind, emotion, and will to Him. As those who are regenerated, we have to learn that we cannot go along with our own mind, emotion, and will, for they are old and natural. Rather, we must deny them.

PRACTICING TO DENY THE NATURAL MIND, EMOTION, AND WILL

A number of believers genuinely experience the Holy Spirit when they pray. But after they pray, they remain in the old mind, old emotion, and old will. Although it seems that in their times of prayer they are in the spirit, after their prayer, they are in the natural mind, emotion, and will. These ones do not know how to live by Christ and deny their mind, emotion, and will. If you are going to experience Christ, the first lesson you have to learn is that of rejecting and denying your natural mind, emotion, and will. This point cannot be emphasized enough. If you deny the natural mind, emotion, and will, the Holy Spirit within your spirit will take over these parts of your being. To be a Christian is to live a life in which we do not live by the mind, emotion, and will, but instead live by Christ in the spirit.

A sister once came to me and said, "Brother Lee, my temper is very bad. As a wife and mother in a family, my bad temper hurts others. It was because of my temper's ill effect on my husband and family that I believed in the Lord. I believed that He would deliver me from my bad temper. But even though I have been saved, I cannot overcome my bad temper." After telling me these things, she asked me what she should do. It is very hard to help people overcome their temper. I said to her, "Sister, do you realize that since you are regenerated, Christ lives within you?" She answered that she did. I continued, "If you go along with your emotion, it will be very hard for you to overcome your temper. If you go along with Christ, it will be very easy for you to overcome your temper. With what will you go along? There are two possibilities. Will you go along with your emotion, or will you go along with Christ? If you go along with your emotion, you must be prepared to lose your temper. If, however, you go along with Christ, you will surely overcome your temper. You have the emotion and you have Christ. Which one will you go along with?" She replied, "Brother Lee, I realize that I must go along with Christ instead of going along with my emotion." I asked her if she really meant this—if she would actually go along with Christ instead of with her natural emotion. She was unable to answer. This sister realized her problem was that since the time she had been regenerated, she had not practiced going along with Christ. Instead, she still went along with her own emotion with the hope that Christ would help her overcome her temper. This sister's experience points to a principle: you cannot go along with your emotion and at the same time hope that Christ will help you overcome it. You have to give up one or the other. If you go along with your emotion, you must give up Christ; if you go along with Christ, you must give up your emotion. When I explained this to her, she told me that she was clear. Nevertheless, I continued, "Sister, you are clear, but you need some practice. You are quite accustomed to going along with your emotion, but you are not used to going along with Christ. You have to practice going along with Christ." The sister took my word and practiced. After some time she came back to me and said, "Brother Lee, I practiced going along with Christ. But many times I forgot to go along with Christ and instead went along with my emotion." I responded, "Sister, you are a Christian. As such, whenever you are going to do something, you must first check to see whether it is according to Christ or according to your emotion. In everything, check and pray. Do not pray that the Lord would help you overcome your temper; pray rather that you would go along with the Lord and give up your emotion. Practice by praying."

Our need is to practice. We are fellowshipping concerning how to experience, enjoy, and apply Christ in a very practical way. In our daily life, we should always practice going along with Christ, on the one hand, and giving up our mind, emotion, and will, on the other hand. If we practice this—the daily giving up of our mind, emotion, and will and going along with Christ—the Spirit, who is the reality of Christ, will occupy our mind, emotion, and will. In other words, Christ will make His home in our heart. Then our entire being—mind, emotion, and will—will be full of Christ. To practice this is the way for us to experience Christ practically in our daily life.

There is no need for us to pay much attention to the sinful matters in our lives. We do not need to try to overcome our sins. Our only need is to practice going along with Christ, denying our mind, emotion, and will, and giving our heart wholly to Christ. When we do this, Christ will take our heart and make it His home. This is the renewing of the mind, the renewing of the emotion, and the renewing of the will—the transformation of our whole being.

We have been regenerated in our spirit. Now we have to be transformed in our mind, emotion, and will. We do this by practicing to always go along with Christ and always deny our natural mind, emotion, and will. This is a great part of the work of the Holy Spirit. This is not merely some sort of teaching; nor is this a matter of merely being filled with or baptized in the Holy Spirit. This is something we must practice day by day in all aspects of our life. After we have been filled with the Holy Spirit and baptized by Him, every moment of every day for the rest of our lives we have to practice denying our natural mind, emotion, and will and going along with Christ. The unbelievers can never practice this because they do not have Christ as the Spirit within them. However, we do, and He is waiting for us to go along with Him. Again—and I stress this very much—we must reject and deny the natural mind, the natural will, and the natural emotion and go along with the Christ who indwells us. We have to love Him with a sincere and single heart. Day by day we should tell the Lord that we love Him. When we do, we must realize that the real, sincere love for Him is shown in our denial of ourselves. We go along with the Lord because we love Him. To go along with Him simply means to deny ourselves.

As an illustration, let us say that I am serving the Lord with a brother. As a Christian, I have to practice the day-by-day and moment-by-moment denial of my natural mind, natural emotion, and natural will. This is to go along with my Lord, whom I love. If I do not deny myself and do not go along with the Lord and instead remain in my old mind, emotion, and will, it may take only one week before the brother and I part ways. This is because in my natural emotion, I may not feel happy with him. If I am to go on with this brother and serve with him in a proper way, I have no choice but to deny my natural mind, emotion, and will and go along with the indwelling Christ. The problem is not the relationship between the brother and me; the problem is the relationship between me and the Lord Jesus. If I go along with the Lord, I will be at peace with my brother. However, if I do not go along with the Lord and instead go along with myself and my natural emotion, I will no doubt leave the brother. As Christians, we all have to practice rejecting our mind, emotion, and will and going along with the Christ who is making home in our hearts.

Simply praying, being filled with the Holy Spirit, and believing that Christ lives within us is not enough. We have to practice denying our mind, emotion, and will and going along with Christ. This will renew our mind, our emotion, and our will, transforming our whole being into Christ's image (2 Cor. 3:18). It is not enough that we have been regenerated in our spirit. We need to be transformed in our soul. Christ is in our spirit, awaiting a chance to take over our whole being. He is always waiting. We only need to give Him the opportunity. I am afraid that although many of us love the Lord very much, we still do not know how to experience Christ. The way to experience Christ is very simple. Every day, moment by moment, we need only to practice one thing—denying our mind, emotion, and will to go along with the indwelling Christ.

THE PRACTICAL WAY TO DENY THE SOUL AND GO ALONG WITH THE INDWELLING CHRIST—GOING ALONG WITH OUR REGENERATED SPIRIT

At this point, you may ask me how we can practically go along with Christ. To answer this question, we need only remember that Christ is in our spirit (2 Tim. 4:22; 2 Cor. 13:5). Instead of going along with our mind, emotion, and will, we should go along with our spirit. To go along with our spirit is actually to go along with Christ because Christ is in our spirit. We should not think that Christ is only in the heavens. Christ today is also in our spirit (Rom. 8:34, 10). Hence, to go along with our spirit is the practical way to deny the soul and go along with Christ.

I have had many difficult experiences with various brothers over the years. In such situations, I have gone to the Lord and told Him, "Lord here I am. I know that I cannot go along with my mind, emotion, and will. I know that I must go along with You by going along with my spirit. My spirit tells me that I have to be one with this brother, but my will has already made the decision to leave him. Lord, what shall I do? Should I go along with my decision—with my will—or should I go along with You who indwell my spirit?" Although in my spirit the Lord has already answered my question and my innermost part tells me that I have to stay with this dear brother, my will is stubborn, having already made a decision to leave him. In such a situation, what shall I do? This is a lesson for us as Christians. Will we go along with our will or will we go along with the spirit? Many times we have to tell the Lord, even with tears in our eyes, "Lord, I cannot go along with my will. I have to go along with You." It is not enough for us simply to praise the Lord that He is our life, for we still have our natural mind, natural emotion, and natural will. We must learn the lesson of giving up the mind, emotion, and will to go along with the spirit, where Christ lives.

Having been regenerated in our spirit, our need is to go along with our spirit and to forget, deny, and reject our mind, emotion, and will. This is very simple, but it needs our daily practice. I assure you that the more we practice this, the more we will experience Christ day by day and the more Christ will be real, close, dear, and rich to us. The more we practice this, the more we will have the experience of Christ in a rich and sweet way. Sometimes our enjoyment will be so sweet that our tears will flow. Then we will help people know and experience Christ not just in teaching but in real experience. This is what we need today. We do not need more teachings or doctrines; we need the real practice of experiencing Christ in the spirit. This way is simple, but it needs our practice. I am deeply burdened concerning this simple way, and I offer it to you for your practice.

Chapter Five

OUR NEED TO BE FILLED WITH CHRIST

Scripture Reading: Col. 2:9-10; Eph. 3:19

Colossians 2:9-10 says, "For in Him dwells all the fullness of the Godhead bodily, and you have been made full in Him, who is the Head of all rule and authority." These two verses say first that the fullness of the Godhead dwells in Christ. Then they say that we are made full in this Christ. We are made full through the fullness of the Godhead which dwells in Christ. Because the fullness is in Christ, we can be made full in Him.

Ephesians 3:19 says, "And to know the knowledge-surpassing love of Christ, that you may be filled unto all the fullness of God." For us to be filled unto all the fullness of God means that we are filled to overflowing with all the riches of Christ (cf. Eph. 3:8). To be filled unto all the fullness of God is to be filled with the riches of Christ to the point that we express His riches. The expression of the riches is the fullness. This verse and the aforementioned verses in Colossians speak concerning the same matter.

In this chapter, we come to a matter for which I have been heavily burdened for some time. As Christians, we must realize that we are not perfect—full and complete—by creation. For this reason we need to be regenerated. The Scriptures tell us that we are vessels made to contain God (Rom. 9:23; cf. Gen. 1:26). A vessel of any kind can never be perfect or complete by itself. Until a vessel is filled with the content for which it was made, it will not be perfect. Although a cup may seem perfect by itself, as long as it is empty, it is not perfect. We are vessels, and as such, we are not perfect by ourselves.

Many of us pay too much attention to the negative side of the Christian life and neglect the positive side. We talk too much about how to overcome sins and the world while neglecting the positive matters. One of the main positive matters of the Christian life is that of being filled unto all the fullness of God. The normal Christian life is one of being filled with Christ and His riches. We must be saturated and permeated by Christ so that we can have the image of Christ (Rom. 8:29). Even if we are victorious over sin and the world yet are not filled with Christ and do not have His image, we as vessels are empty and thus not perfect. If we pay attention to the positive side of the Christian life, the negative matters will naturally, automatically, and spontaneously be taken care of. If we are filled with Christ, we will overcome sin and the world. Let us therefore stress the positive side and pay less attention to the negative side.

We need to be perfected; that is, we need to be filled unto all the fullness of God. Our main problem today is not sin and the world but the fact that we are short of Christ. If we are short of Christ, we will experience many troubles. We can liken this to being malnourished. If we are short of vitamins, germs will be able to trouble us. If, on the other hand, we are full of vitamins, we can be assured that the germs' effect will be nullified. When it comes to health, we would do well to not be overly anxious about germs and simply increase our intake of vitamins. In the same way, when it comes to our Christian life, let us not stress sins, the world, and our weaknesses. Let us instead set our eyes on the heavenly Christ and be filled with His unsearchable riches.

We need Christ. However I am afraid that we have the wrong concept of what it means to need Christ. We may think that we need Christ primarily to comfort and help us. While that may be true, in a deeper and more important sense, we need Christ to fill us until we are full of Him. Until we are full of Him, we are short of something and therefore empty and not perfect. For this reason, we need to be filled with Christ. We have to have a revelation concerning Christ. The concept we have of Christ is too narrow and limited. If the Lord would open our eyes and give us the heavenly vision in full, we would realize that Christ is our perfection and completeness. We have to realize that we are empty vessels—containers without content. In this state, we can never be complete, full, and perfect. Our need is not victory over sin, deliverance from the world, hope, or peace; our need is Christ. We need nothing but Christ. Even if we as vessels are clean, pure, and entirely victorious over sins and the world, if we are devoid of Christ, we are still empty. We need to experience Christ so that we are made perfect, complete, and full in Him.

We all need to be deeply impressed with the fact that we need Christ. Some may say that we need sanctification, holiness, and other spiritual matters. However, the sanctification and holiness we need are actually just Christ Himself (1 Cor. 1:30). Others may tell us that we need strength, energy, and power. In actuality, however, the strength, energy, and power we need are Christ (Isa. 12:2; 1 Cor. 1:24). At heart, our need is not for various things, regardless of how spiritual they may be; our need is simply Christ. I was a Christian for over fifteen years before I realized this. One day God opened my eyes and gave me the revelation that I need nothing but Christ. We may think that we are short of many things, but we are short only of Christ. Even if we have no sin, as long as we are empty, we are not perfect. By creation itself, we are not perfect and are still short of something. We were made as vessels to be filled with Christ. Until Christ fills us, we are lacking and are not perfected. We need to realize deeply, clearly, and definitely that we are but empty vessels. No matter how good, pure, clean, and beautiful we are, we are still empty if Christ does not fill us. I repeat this again and again: we need Christ. Without Him, we are empty vessels.

Not only do we need to see that we are empty vessels; we also need to see what kind of vessel we are in the first place. A teacup is a vessel, albeit a very simple one, for it has only one part. Once a cup is filled with tea, it is full and complete. We, too, are vessels. Our glorious and mysterious God needs a vessel. However the vessel He needs is not as simple as a teacup. The most complicated matter in God's creation is the human being. In Psalm 51 David said, "Behold, You delight in truth in the inward parts; / And in the hidden part You would make known wisdom to me" (v. 6). According to this verse, we have both the inward parts and the hidden part. The inward parts must be the parts of the soul—the mind, the emotion, and the will (Heb. 8:10; Jer. 31:33; cf. 1 Thes. 5:23). Likewise, the hidden part must be the spirit—composed of the conscience, fellowship, and intuition (Rom. 9:1; 8:16; Eph. 6:18; 1 Cor. 2:11; Mark 2:8)—for it is the most hidden part within us. The heart, being a composition of the inward parts and the hidden part, is composed of the three parts of the soul plus the conscience in the spirit. As human beings, therefore, we are very complicated vessels.

As we vessels consider our complicated being, we must ask ourselves how much Christ is in our inward parts. In the Bible, we are told that we should have the mind of Christ and that Christ should make His home in our hearts (1 Cor. 2:16; Eph. 3:17). But how much is Christ in our mind and in our heart? How much is Christ in the parts of our soul? Any part that is not full of Christ is not perfect. If we do not have enough Christ in our mind, our mind has yet to be perfected. If we do not have enough Christ in our emotion, our emotion is not perfect. Likewise with the will—if Christ does not permeate our will, then our will is not perfect. The converse is also true. The perfect mind is a mind that is full of Christ, the perfect emotion is an emotion that is full of Christ, and the perfect will is a will that is full of Christ. Hence, the parts of our vessel can be made perfect only by Christ. Christ Himself is the perfection of our mind, emotion, and will. The heart that is full of Christ is a perfect heart. If it is without Christ, our heart—though it may be pure, clean, right, and good—is short of Christ and is thus empty and not perfect.

My burden is not to give you much doctrine. My burden is to help you realize that Christ is our completeness, perfection, and that we are made full in Him. If you are short of Christ in any part, you are not complete. Your entire inner being—the inward parts and the hidden part—have to be filled with Christ in order for you to be made complete. You only need Christ. You must forget about all other things.

LIVING A CHRISTIAN LIFE BY BEING FILLED WITH CHRIST

Today many people misinterpret the Bible. They take the Bible as a book of proper behavior and morality. Although the Bible does speak of morality, we must realize that the Bible's central point is Christ, who fills us and in whom we are made full. The Bible tells us that we have to love one another (1 John 4:7). Real love, however, is not simply human affection. Genuine love is the overflow of Christ as love from within us to others. Many verses also tell us that we have to be humble (Matt. 23:12; 1 Pet. 5:5-6). To be humble is to be full of Christ and to have this Christ flow out of us (cf. Phil. 2:8, 5). Consequently, when we are full of Christ, we will be very humble. The Bible also tells us that Christians must obey their parents. Ephesians 6:1 says, "Children, obey your parents in the Lord, for this is right." When reading this verse, we generally forget the little phrase *in the Lord.* We have to obey our parents, but we must do it in the Lord. This simply means that we need to be filled with Christ. Only then will we be able to obey our parents. The obedience we render to our parents is actually the overflow of Christ from within our being. In the Scriptures we are also told that we have to sacrifice, that is, give up, everything we have (Rom. 12:1; 2 Cor. 12:15). The sacrifice about which the Bible speaks is the overflow of Christ. It is because we have been filled with Christ and are full of Christ that we spontaneously give up all things. It should be clear that the Bible speaks mainly of Christ filling us, making us full of Him, and then flowing out of us. Our need is to be filled with and to overflow Christ.

In 1937 I was preaching the gospel to some learned students in Nanking, China. On one such occasion, a very well-educated and intelligent young woman came to me and said, "I appreciate your preaching very much and would like to receive it. However, I am fond of watching movies. I am wondering whether or not I will be allowed to go to movies if I become a Christian." Her question had the potential of being somewhat troublesome. On the one hand, I dared not tell her that after she became a Christian she could go to the movies as she liked. On the other hand, I could not tell her that she would no longer be allowed to attend movies. This young woman loved the movies so much simply because she was empty. If she were filled with Christ, she would not have any room in her being for movies. I illustrated this principle to her in the following way. I said, "Let us say that there is a child here with a very sharp knife in his hand. Of course, we realize the danger that the knife poses to the child. What would you do to get the knife out of this child's hand?" The woman replied, "Mr. Lee, this is quite easy. We simply place several pieces of fruit or candy on the floor. When the child sees the treats, he will put down the knife and take them up instead. Both of his hands will be full of the treats. Then, even if we ask him to take up the knife again, he would reply that since his hands are full of better things, he would not." When this young woman had finished answering, I said to her, "You are right. When you are full of Christ, you will no longer need movies. This is the Christian faith. Being a Christian is not a matter of giving up movies or many other things. Being a Christian is simply a matter of being filled with Christ." We all must realize this. Being a Christian is simply a matter of being filled with Christ.

THE PRACTICAL WAY TO BE FILLED WITH CHRIST—PRAYER

How then can we be filled with Christ? To answer this, we must have a further realization. On the one hand, we are empty vessels. On the other hand, we are occupied vessels. If we are full of Christ, that is wonderful. However, if we are occupied by something other than Christ, we have a great need. It is because we are not filled with Christ but are filled with other matters that we stand in need of the present message. Too many things other than Christ occupy our mind, emotion, will, and heart. Each of us knows what occupies us. It is pitiful that we are filled with things other than Christ. When we find that this is our case, we simply have to come to Christ and tell Him that we are full of things other than Him. This is not so much confession as it is simply telling Him our case. How we need to go to Christ to tell Him how much we have been filled with other things! Our need, I must repeat, is to simply tell Him how much our mind has been occupied by things other than Him.

Many Christians pray largely in vain. This is due mainly to the fact that they do not speak the truth to the Lord. Even though they are occupied with many things other than the Lord, they never admit this to the Lord. Although they may tell the Lord many other things, such as how weak they are and how much they need strengthening and power, these prayers are for the most part vain because they are not sincere. Sincere prayer is prayer in which we go to the Lord and tell Him how much we have been occupied in the past and how much we continue to be occupied at present. We need to tell the Lord the truth. We must tell Him, "Lord, I am still occupied by these things in my mind and by those things in my emotion and will." This is sincere prayer. If we pray in this way, the more we tell the Lord, the more the Lord will occupy our mind, emotion, and will. The more we pray to the Lord in this way, the more He will occupy our entire heart and make our heart a home for Himself.

If we take this way, everything will be wonderful and glorious. If there is the need to love others, the overflow of Christ from within our being will be the love toward others. If there is the need to be humble, the overflow of Christ from within will be the humility. Christ Himself will fill us and meet our need. This is the right way to be a Christian. I know many saints who have been troubled by the enemy tempting them by saying, "You say that you love the Lord. Therefore, you should be able to be humble and love others." If we give in to Satan's temptation of being humble and loving in ourselves, we will be defeated by him immediately. Whenever the enemy challenges us in such a way, we should tell him, "I do not know whether I can be humble or love others. But one thing I know: I want to be filled with Christ. I do not know anything else. The only thing that I want is to be filled with Christ. Christ is my perfection. Christ is my completeness. Christ is my fullness. He will take care of everything else for me."

We need to learn to be filled with Christ by praying to the Lord genuinely and honestly. Christ is the Spirit, and as such He is in our spirit (2 Cor. 3:17; 2 Tim. 4:22). Christ is so real in our spirit. The way for us to be filled with Christ is to simply go to Him with a sincere heart, open our spirit to Him, and tell Him how much we are occupied in our mind, emotion, will, and heart with things other than Him. Let us tell Him the truth. Let us tell Him the real situation from our heart. Then we will be filled with Him. Day by day, we need to pray in such a way.

QUESTIONS AND ANSWERS

Question: Many Christians speak of living by the Holy Spirit with power. Is this synonymous with being filled with Christ?

The current teaching in much of Christianity concerning the Holy Spirit frustrates our ability to see clearly the matter of being filled with Christ. We have to realize that in the New Testament age, there are two aspects concerning the Holy Spirit. The first aspect of the Holy Spirit is that the Spirit is the Spirit of life. We find this term in Romans 8:2: "For the law of the Spirit of life has freed me in Christ Jesus from the law of sin and of death." The second aspect of the Holy Spirit is that the Spirit is the Spirit of power. Regarding the Holy Spirit as the Spirit of life, the New Testament uses the prepositions *in* or *within* (Rom. 8:9, 11; 1 Cor. 3:16; 2 Tim. 1:14). Regarding the Holy Spirit as the Spirit of power, the New Testament uses the prepositions *on* or *upon* (Acts 1:8; 10:44; 19:6). As the Spirit of life, the Spirit is within us; as the Spirit of power, the Spirit is upon us. John 14:17 says, "Even the Spirit of reality, whom the world cannot receive, because it does not behold Him or know Him; but you know Him, because He abides with you and shall be in you." Because we know that the Gospel of John deals much with life, the Spirit mentioned in this book must be the Spirit of life. Hence, this verse tells us that the Spirit—the Spirit of life—is *in* us. Again, John 7:37-39 says, "Now on the last day, the great day of the feast, Jesus stood and cried out, saying, If anyone thirsts, let him come to Me and drink. He who believes into Me, as the Scripture said, out of his innermost being shall flow rivers of living water. But this He said concerning the Spirit, whom those who believed into Him were about to receive; for the Spirit was not yet, because Jesus had not yet been glorified." From this passage, we can realize that the Spirit mentioned here is the living water which we can drink and which can be within us. While in these verses in John the Spirit is said to be in us and is likened to water that we can drink, Luke 24:49 speaks of the other aspect of the Spirit: "And behold, I send forth the promise of My Father upon you; but as for you, stay in the city until you put on power from on high." Some translations render it as *are clothed*. To be clothed with power refers to the Holy Spirit coming *upon* the disciples as the Spirit of power in Acts 1:8. For this reason, the word *clothed* is used here (clothing being *upon* the wearer).

In these verses, we can see two symbols of the Spirit. On one hand, the Spirit is the living water; on the other hand, this Spirit is clothing. As the living water, we drink Him; as the clothing, we put Him on. We must take in the Spirit of life and put on the Spirit of power. The endowment of power, that is, of the Spirit of power, is the Holy Spirit outside of us. This outpouring of the Holy Spirit upon us is like rain and is something that takes place outside of us. The Spirit of life, however, must be taken in by us.

We can see this in many other portions of the Bible as well. On the evening of His resurrection, Jesus came to the disciples and breathed *into* them, telling them to receive the Holy Spirit (John 20:22). Then on the day of Pentecost, the Holy Spirit came down *upon* the disciples as a wind and filled the whole house (Acts 2:2). Here we see two more symbols—breath and wind. The breath is for life, and the wind is for power. On the day of the Lord's resurrection, the disciples received the Spirit of life as breath into them. Fifty days later, the Spirit of power came upon them as wind. The symbols of the living water and the breath are both spoken of in the Gospel of John, which deals with the matter of life. In the Gospel of John, in which the Spirit is mainly the Spirit of life, the symbols of the Spirit of life are breath and living water. In the books by Luke, however—the Gospel of Luke and Acts—the Spirit as the Spirit of power is symbolized by clothing and wind. These two symbols represent the Spirit's inner aspect of life and outer aspect of power. These are the two aspects of the one Spirit. It is important to realize that when we say that we need to be filled with Christ, we are referring to the inner aspect of the Spirit, the Spirit of life. In order to be filled with Christ, we need to be filled with the Spirit of life. It is not sufficient to be clothed by the Spirit of power; our desperate need is to be filled with the Spirit of life.

We can see these two aspects of the Spirit with the Lord Jesus. The Lord Jesus was born of the Holy Spirit (Matt. 1:18, 20). Hence, even before He was baptized with water, He was filled with the Holy Spirit. However, after He was baptized with water, the Holy Spirit came down upon Him (3:16; John 1:32). From the verses related to His birth, we know that this does not mean that before His water baptism He did not have the Holy Spirit. The Lord Jesus was born of the Holy Spirit and filled with the Holy Spirit, yet after He was baptized with water, the Holy Spirit came down upon Him. Within, He had already been filled with the Holy Spirit, yet in order to minister, He needed to be endowed with the Spirit of power without.

Today we have to realize that we need the two aspects of the work of the Holy Spirit—the inner aspect and the outer aspect. The inner aspect is to be filled with the Spirit of life, and the outer aspect is to be endowed with the Spirit of power.

Question: Colossians 3:1 tells us to seek the things which are above. What are some of those things?

The things which are above are the heavenly things, including the ascended Christ and all things pertaining to Him. This verse tells us to seek the things which are above; however, if we are not filled with Christ, we will not have the power to seek those things. After creating man, the first thing God did in relation to man was not to take care of man's work but to take care of man's eating. God knows that if man does not eat, he cannot work. For example, we must eat breakfast before we can work in the morning, eat lunch before we can work in the afternoon, and eat dinner before we can come to the meeting in the evening. Because we can do nothing without first eating, eating is of primary importance and must consequently be our first priority. Spiritually speaking, to eat is to be filled with Christ as our spiritual food. After God created man, He took care of everything so that man could eat the proper food. God's intention was that man would eat God in Christ as the tree of life (Gen. 2:9; John 15:1; 11:25). His intention remains the same today. In John 6:57, the Lord Jesus said, "As the living Father has sent Me and I live because of the Father, so he who eats Me, he also shall live because of Me." Only when we eat Christ, are filled by Him, and are satisfied with Him are we able to do many things. If we are starving to death, we can do nothing, regardless of what we intend or declare. When we are filled and satisfied with Christ, we have the energy to work. Hence, our primary concern and our first need is to be filled with Christ. Let us forget about sins, the world, our deeds, and our works, and simply be filled with Christ. Only then will we be able to seek the things which are above.